The Naturalist Intelligence

Karen Roth

TRAINING AND PUBLISHING, INC.

The Naturalist Intelligence

Published by SkyLight Training and Publishing, Inc.
2626 S. Clearbrook Dr., Arlington Heights, IL 60005-5310
800-348-4474, 847-290-6600
Fax 847-290-6609
info@iriskylight.com
http://www.iriskylight.com

Creative Director: Robin Fogarty
Managing Editor: Ela Aktay
Editor: Amy Kinsman
Proofreader: Sue Schumer
Acquisitions Editor: Jean Ward
Book Designer: Donna Ramirez
Type Compositor: Donna Ramirez
Cover Illustrator: David Stockman
Production Supervisor: Bob Crump

ISBN 1-57517-078-7

2208C-7-98
Item no. 1584
06 05 04 03 02 01 00 99 98   15 14 13 12 11 10 9 8 7 6 5 4 3

Contents

The Naturalist Intelligence

In 1983, with his landmark book, *Frames of Mind*, Howard Gardner introduced his theory of multiple intelligences. It changed the whole way of looking at how people are smart. Howard Gardner has added an eighth intelligence, the naturalist, to his original list of seven: verbal/linguistic, musical/rhythmic, logical/mathematical, visual/spatial, bodily/kinesthetic, interpersonal, and intrapersonal. Robin Fogarty best defines these intelligences in her book *Brain Compatible Classrooms:*

> The *visual/spatial intelligence* comprises the abilities to visually depict and appreciate information and ideas. Embedded in the *verbal/linguistic intelligence* is the gift of language and literacy. The *logical/mathematical intelligence* houses the abilities to reason and think in abstractions. The *musical/rhythmic intelligence* gives one the sense of melody, rhythm, and rhyme. The *bodily/kinesthetic intelligence* is manifested in the muscle memory of the body. The charismatic leader, the sympathetic counselor, and empathic social worker epitomize the interrelational character of the *interpersonal intelligence.* The intelligence named the *intrapersonal intelligence* is found in the inner nature and soul of the person—the inner thought or reflective self. (1997, p. 171–173)

When Gardner was asked why this eighth intelligence was added, he said that he had been asked to explain the achievements of the great biologists such as Charles Darwin and of people who had a real mastery of taxonomy, who understood about different species, and who could recognize patterns in nature, classify objects, and quickly grasp relationships in ecosystems. When he tried to explain this kind of ability, he found he would have to "manipulate the other intelligences in ways that weren't appropriate" (Checkley 1997, p.8).

This inability to fit individuals gifted in natural science into his original system of intelligences prompted Gardner to explore further. Using the same criteria and investigative process he used in identifying the first seven intelligences, Gardner found that naturalist intelligence passed with flying colors. Some of the reasons Gardner gives for identifying the naturalist as a separate intelligence are "First, it's an intelligence we need to survive as human beings. We need, for example, to know which animals to hunt and which to run away from. Second, this ability isn't restricted to human beings. Other animals need to have a naturalist intelligence to survive. Finally, the big selling point is that brain evidence supports the existence of the naturalist intelligence. There are certain parts of the brain particularly dedicated to the recognition and the naming of what are called 'natural' things" (Checkley 1997, pp. 8–9).

> ... Gardner does not see the present eight intelligences as exhaustive.

Having identified this eighth intelligence, Gardner is still keeping the door open to the possibility of the identification of additional intelligences. Gardner originally began to investigate and identify multiple intelligences as a result of his dissatisfaction with the concept of IQ as a general capacity or potential which every human being possesses to a greater or lesser extent. He was additionally dissatisfied with assumptions that human intelligence could be measured by standardized verbal instruments. He asks that people consider a far wider and more universal set of competencies than has ordinarily been considered and which do not lend themselves to measurement by standard verbal methods. Because of this pluralistic view of intelligence, Gardner does not see the present eight intelligences as exhaustive. He says he would be surprised if they were. He also emphasizes that he would only identify an intelligence as one of the multiple intelligences if it met certain biological and psychological specifications. These specifications, defined later, are the eight "signs" or criteria Gardner uses to identify the intelligences.

Defined by Gardner

When Gardner set about to investigate a more expanded view of intelligence, his prerequisites for an intelligence were that "a human intellectual competence must entail a set of skills of problem solving—enabling the individual *to resolve genuine problems or difficulties* that he or she encounters and, when appropriate, to create an effective product—and must also entail the potential for *finding or creating problems*—thereby laying the groundwork for the acquisition of knowledge" (Gardner 1983, p. 60–61). These prerequisites represent Gardner's efforts to focus on the "intellectual strengths that prove of some importance within a cultural context" (Gardner 1983, p. 61). This is a definition that guides Gardner's identification of multiple intelligences.

The naturalist intelligence, as defined by Gardner, "designates the human ability to discriminate among living things (plants, animals) as well as sensitivity to other features of the natural world (clouds, rock configurations)" (Checkley 1997, p. 12). He places the development of this intelligence in context of evolution from need. This ability was clearly of value in the evolutionary past of humans as hunters, gatherers, and farmers, and it continues to be central in such roles as botanist or chef. In the current application Gardner adds, "I also speculate that much of the consumer society exploits the naturalist intelligence, which can be mobilized in the discrimination among cars, sneakers, kinds of makeup, and the like. The kind of pattern recognition valued in certain of the sciences may also draw upon naturalist intelligence" (Checkley 1997, p. 12).

Gardner identifies individuals of naturalist intelligence both within and without cultures "with science."

Gardner identifies individuals of naturalist intelligence both within and without cultures "with science." In cultures without scientists and biologists, he points to persons skilled in the application of folk taxonomies as naturalists who recognize and categorize specimens in terms of current formal taxonomies. He identifies John James Audubon and Roger Torrey Peterson as naturalists whose knowledge of the living world is outstanding, as well as those individuals who study organisms in a more theoretical way such as Charles Darwin, Ernst Mayr, and E. O. Wilson.

Most people can recognize such things as types of trees, cats, and dogs. There are some individuals who, from a very early age, can recognize and classify artifacts with great precision and accuracy. Many educators know of young students who know all there is to know about dinosaurs, butterflies, fish, rocks, etc. They have a deep interest and fascination with something in nature and are driven to investigate and become an "expert" in a particular natural subject. These are the students who exhibit naturalist intelligence.

The Eight Criteria Applied to the Naturalist Intelligence

In identifying the original seven intelligences, Gardner used a set of criteria against which he measured and determined the validity of each intelligence. While he admits that all eight of the criteria may not be present in each intelligence, the majority are. He emphasizes that ". . . the selection (or rejection) of a candidate intelligence is reminiscent of an artistic judgment than of a scientific assessment" (Gardner 1983, p. 63). He sees the procedure "as a kind of subjective factor analysis" (Gardner 1983, p. 63). The scientific part of this process, according to Gardner, is that he makes his findings public so that other investigators are able to review them and draw their own conclusions.

Gardner's eight criteria for the existence of an intelligence are the following:

1. **Potential Isolation by Brain Damage**
   An intelligence is autonomous when it can be obliterated or preserved, in isolation, upon injury to the brain.

   Naturalist example: There are examples in clinical literature of individuals who have brain damage and remain able to recognize and name inanimate objects but lose the capacity to identify and name living things.

2. **The Existence of Prodigies, Mentally Handicapped Individuals With Savant Behaviors, and Other Exceptional Individuals**
   The particular intelligence can be scrutinized in isolation. The super-occurrence or total absence of a faculty in itself suggests in the very existence of that intelligence.

Naturalist example: Charles Darwin is a example of a prodigy who had an early fascination with plants and animals and was driven to identify, classify, and interact with them. There are also individuals who are impaired in this ability.

3. **An Identifiable Core Operation or a Set of Operations**
An intelligence is sparked by certain kinds of stimuli inherent to the particular area of their intelligence.

Naturalist example: Gardner is not certain just which neural centers are involved in the naturalist intelligence. It may depend on whether the information is recognized from illustration or direct interaction. But because the human naturalist ability appears closely related to that of other animals, he thinks, with more study, it should be possible to identify which brain centers are involved.

4. **A Distinctive Developmental History, Along With a Definable Set of Expert "End State" Performances**
Each intelligence presents a traceable path toward proficiency in a specific realm from basic to complex.

Naturalist example: Gardner has identified several "end states" or logical professions arising from the naturalist intelligence, including biologist, hunter, farmer, gardener, chef. All of these "end states" have a developmental path from basic to proficient skills.

5. **An Evolutionary History and Evolutionary Plausibility**
An intelligence becomes more credible if it has some evolutionary roots that can be traced to the present from an earlier need.

Naturalist example: The evolutionary history of the naturalist intelligence is evidenced by the ability of a species to adapt to its environment to survive, using the ability to determine predators and prey.

6. **Support From Experimental Psychological Tasks**
   Demonstration of a particular intelligence can be documented by the experiments of cognitive psychologists.

   Naturalist example: Gardner asserts that psychologists haven't shown much interest in the naturalist ability, but there is some evidence in the literature to show the existence of special psychological mechanisms that identify natural things, such as birds, trees, etc.

7. **Support From Psychometric Findings**
   Standardized tests can provide explicit evidence of the existence of an intelligence and add to its reliability and validity.

   Naturalist example: Standardized biology tests are able to measure the ability to identify and classify flora and fauna.

8. **Susceptibility in Encoding in a Symbol System**
   The intelligence can be encoded into universally understood symbols, such as language, picturing, mathematics, etc).

   Naturalist example: There is evidence of linguistic and taxonomy systems that exist in every culture for classifying plants and animals.

Based upon the above review of the naturalist intelligence using the eight criteria, Gardner added this eighth intelligence to the list of multiple intelligences.

Application of the Naturalist Intelligence

Now that the naturalist intelligence has been added to the list of multiple intelligences, educators want to know how to incorporate it into their instructional strategies for the multiple intelligences classroom.

Two charts from Robin Fogarty's *Problem-Based Learning and Other Curricular Models for the Multiple Intelligences Classroom* are particularly helpful.

Ways to Experience Learning (Figure 1) identifies the behaviors of relating, discovering, uncovering, observing, digging, planting, comparing, displaying, and sorting as examples of the types of skills a teacher would have to help his or her students develop to nurture the naturalist intelligence.

Types of Activities (Figure 2) lists specific activities a teacher could use to have students use their naturalist intelligence. The activities include: field trips (farm/zoo), field studies, bird watching, observing nests, planting, photographing, nature walks, forecasting weather, stargazing, fishing, exploring caves, categorizing rocks, ecology studies, catching butterflies, shell collecting, and identifying plants. (Note: While these activities focus on natural subjects, it is also possible to have students use skills of categorizing, classifying, and identifying patterns with urban subjects such as cars, music, clothing, etc.)

Fogarty's book also presents six curricular frameworks (Figure 3) for problem-based learning developed with Gardner's theory of multiple intelligences: problem-based learning, case studies, thematic learning, project learning, service learning, and performance learning. Each model is designed with multidimensional strategies and versatile tools that help

Ways to Experience Learning

Verbal	Visual	Logical	Musical	Interpersonal	Intrapersonal	Bodily	Naturalist
Reporting	Storyboarding	Reasoning	Singing	Discussing	Journaling	Dancing	Relating
Writing essays	Painting	Collecting	Listening	Responding	Intuiting	Sculpting	Discovering
Creeating	Cartooning	Recording	Playing	Dialoguing	Reflecting	Performing	Uncovering
Reciting	Observing	Analyzing	Composing	Reporting	Logging	Preparing	Observing
Listing	Drawing	Graphing	Audiotaping	Surveying	Mediating	Constructing	Digging
Telling/retelling	Illustrating	Comparing/contrasting	Improvising	Questioning	Studying	Acting	Planting
Listening	Diagraming	Classifying	Attending concerts	Paraphrasing	Rehearsing	Role-playing	Comparing
Labeling	Depicting	Ranking	Selecting Music	Clarifying	Self-assessing	Dramatizing	Displaying
Joking	Showing	Evaluating	Critiquing music	Affirming	Expressing	Pantomiming	Sorting

(From *Problem-Based Learning & Other Curriculum Models*, Robin Fogarty, 1997)

FIGURE 1

Types of Activities

Verbal	Visual	Logical	Musical	Interpersonal	Intrapersonal	Bodily	Naturalist
Symbols	Mosaics	Mazes	Performance	Group projects	Journals	Role-playing	Field trips
Printouts	Paintings	Puzzles	Songs	Group tasks	Meditations	Dramatizing	(farm/zoo)
Debates	Drawings	Outlines	Musicals	Observation charts	Self-assessments	Skits	Field studies
Poetry	Sketches	Matrices	Instruments	Social interactions	Intuiting	Body language	Bird watching
Jokes	Illustrations	Sequences	Rhythms	Dialogs	Logs	Facial	Observing nests
Speeches	Cartoons	Patterns	Compositions	Conversations	Records	expressions	Planting
Reading	Sculptures	Logic	Harmonies	Debates	Reflections	Experiments	Photographing
Storytelling	Models	Analogies	Chords	Arguments	Quotations	Dancing	Nature walks
Listening	Constructions	Timelines	Trios/Duos	Consensus	"I Statements"	Gestures	Forecasting
Audiotapes	Maps	Equations	Quartets	Communication	Creative expression	Pantomiming	weather
Essays	Storyboards	Formulas	Beat	Collages	Goals	Field trips	Star gazing
Reports	Videotapes	Theorems	Melodies	Murals	Affirmations	Lab work	Fishing
Crosswords	Photographs	Calculations	Raps	Mosaics	Insight	Interviews	Exploring caves
Fiction	Symbols	Computations	Jingles	Round robins	Poetry	Sports	Categorizing
Nonfiction	Visual aids	Syllogisms	Choral readings	Sports	Interpretations	Games	rocks
Newspapers	Posters	Codes	Scores	Games			Ecology studies
Magazines	Murals	Games	Acappella choirs	Challenges			Catching
Internet	Doodles	Probabilities					butterflies
Research	Statues	Fractions					Shell collecting
Books	Collages						Identifying
Biographies	Mobiles						plants
Bibliographies							

(From *Problem-Based Learning & Other Curriculum Models*, Robin Fogarty, 1997)   **FIGURE 2**

Curricular Models: Phases of Development

Problem-Based Learning	Case Studies	Thematic Learning	Project Learning	Service Learning	Performance Learning
Meeting the problem Defining the problem Gathering the facts • Know • Need to know • Need to do Hypothesizing Researching Rephrasing the problem Generating alternatives Advocating solutions • Probable • Possible • Preferable	Key Concepts Content/Disciplines Compelling narrative Facts Small group discussions Debriefing Follow-up	Brainstorming a bank of themes Posing questions Turning a theme into a problem-solving investigation • Gathering facts • Analyzing the problem • Generating alternatives • Advocating a solution or position	First-story intellect: Gathering activities • Read • Research • Interview • View • Listen • Visit • Search Internet Second-story intellect: Processing activities • Sketch • Draw • Calculate • Generate • Develop a prototype Third-story intellect: Applying activities • Try • Test • Evaluate • Revise • Repeat the cycle • Showcase	Selecting the need for service Finding a community partner Aligning service with educational goals Managing the project • Planning • Monitoring • Evaluating Fostering reflective learning	The Prompt The Vision The Standards The Coaching Context • Explanation • Demonstration • Feedback • Performance • Reflection The Presentation The Reflection

(From *Problem-Based Learning & Other Curriculum Models*, Robin Fogarty, 1997)

FIGURE 3

operationalize Gardner's theory of multiple intelligences. Just as Gardner (1983) emphasizes, the intelligences seldom work in isolation. In holistic learning experiences, they are interrelated to each other. The models in the book provide rich examples of the integration of the multiple intelligences, including the naturalist intelligence.

Just as Gardner (1983) emphasizes, the intelligences seldom work in isolation.

As with the other intelligences, a four-stage model for teaching an intelligence can be found in David Lazear's book *Seven Ways of Teaching.* Lazear uses a four-stage model (Figure 4) to move the learner from an introduction to the intelligence to the transfer of it to other curricular areas and to his or her life outside the classroom. In Stage 1: Awaken, he suggests the naturalist intelligence be triggered by immersing the student in the natural world of plants, animals, water, forests, etc, using the five senses. In Stage II: Amplify, the student learns to distinguish differences and similarities among the same and neighboring species. He also suggests the naturalist intelligence can be enhanced by having students care for pets and growing and nurturing plants. In Stage III: Teach, the student applies the tools of this intelligence (e.g., classifying, discovering, observing) to help learn the academic content, acquire certain specific knowledge and/or skills, and achieve stated outcomes of a particular lesson or unit. In Stage IV: Transfer, the student finds application for the intelligence beyond the classroom. In Lesson Planning Ideas for the Naturalist (Figure 5), Lazear gives several examples across the curriculum for using the tools of the naturalist intelligence.

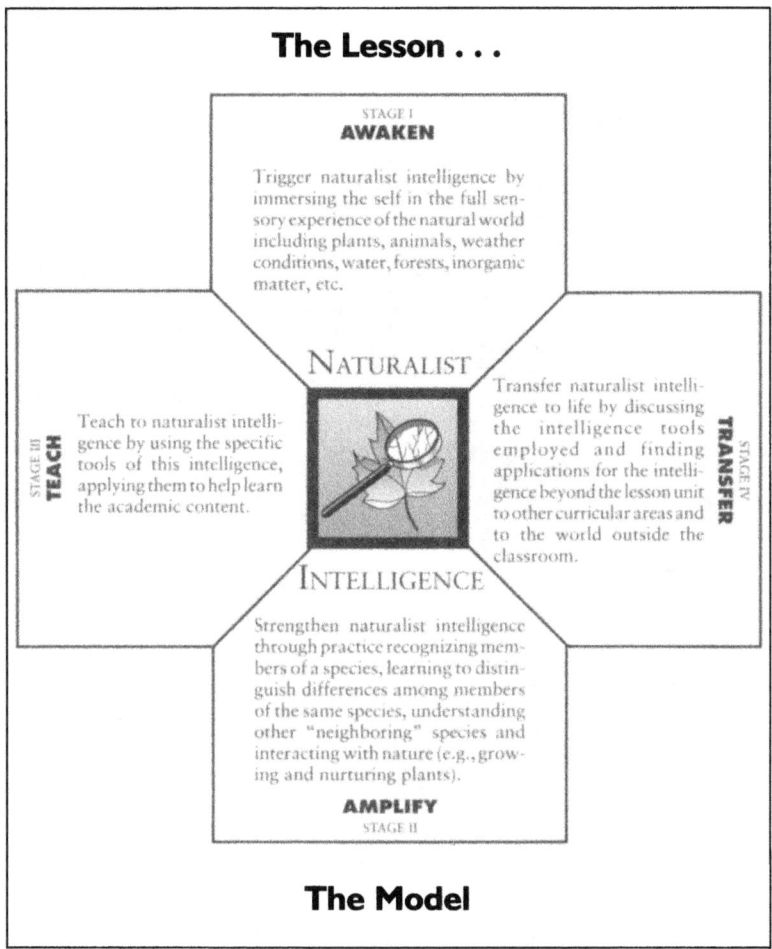

The Lesson . . .

STAGE I
AWAKEN

Trigger naturalist intelligence by immersing the self in the full sensory experience of the natural world including plants, animals, weather conditions, water, forests, inorganic matter, etc.

NATURALIST

STAGE III
TEACH

Teach to naturalist intelligence by using the specific tools of this intelligence, applying them to help learn the academic content.

Transfer naturalist intelligence to life by discussing the intelligence tools employed and finding applications for the intelligence beyond the lesson unit to other curricular areas and to the world outside the classroom.

STAGE IV
TRANSFER

INTELLIGENCE

Strengthen naturalist intelligence through practice recognizing members of a species, learning to distinguish differences among members of the same species, understanding other "neighboring" species and interacting with nature (e.g., growing and nurturing plants).

AMPLIFY
STAGE II

The Model

(Adapted from *Seven Ways of Teaching*, 2nd ed., David Lazear, 1997)

FIGURE 4

Another great resource for ideas for implementing all eight multiple intelligences is James Bellanca's book, *Active Learning Handbook for the Multiple Intelligences Classroom*. The book contains 200 practical, "ready-to-wear" active learning strategies that can be implemented immediately in the K–12 classroom.

LESSON PLANNING IDEAS
Naturalist

Language Arts	Mathematics	Science & Health	Gobal Studies & Geography	History	Fine Arts
Nature scene re-creations/simulations for literature and poetry	Work story problems based on/dealing with patterns in nature	Classify different foods for healthy diet planning	Environmental representations for different cultures	Recognize & interpret historical trends (à la Toynbee)	Compose using sounds from nature & the environment
Poetic/descriptive essay writing based on nature experiences	Use of "nature manipulatives" in math problem-solving	Experience past scientific experiments "first hand" (do them!)	Grow and/or taste foods from various cultures	Understand how "natural events" have influenced history	Recognize and recreate visual iamges of natural patterns
Learn and practice using the vocabulary of nature/the naturalist	Graphic positive/ negative influences on the environment	Keep a diary of the natural processes of your own body	Study the influence of climate/geography on cultural development	Create analogies between historical events & events in nature	Create dances which embody/demonstrate patterns in nature
Understand influences of climate/ environment on authors	Understand the mathematical patterns of nature	Use of various "naturalist taxonomies" on nature field trips	Recreate multi-media experiences of the natural environments of different cultures	Study how animals have effected history & historical trends	Design "full-blown" dramatic enactments of natural process
Creative story-writing using animal characters & their characteristics	Calculation problems based on nature/ natural processes	Use cognitive organizers to explore & understand scientific process	Study animals, insects, etc. from different parts of the world	Study the lives of famous naturalists & their impact on history	Make montages/ collages incorporating "stuff" from nature

(From Seven Ways of Teaching, 2nd ed., David Lazear, 1997)

FIGURE 5

The strategies were selected using the following criteria: a research base to indicate its effectiveness for increasing achievement, support from practicing classroom teachers who have used the strategy with success, and the strategy that was used or observed with students successfully. A few of the strategies from the naturalist chapter include: Gardening Project, Classification Matrix, Plant Observations, Science Exhibition, and Nature Rubbings.

Teachers and students are using the naturalist intelligence in many ways throughout the country.

Teachers and students are using the naturalist intelligence in many ways throughout the country. Some teachers choose environmental themes in an integrated curriculum unit. Many students are involved in the Global Rivers Environmental Education Network (GREEN), based in Ann Arbor, Michigan. GREEN began in the 1980s as a water quality monitoring project in the Great Lakes region and now stresses watershed stewardship across the United States and in 136 countries. Also, in Washington, approximately 1,300 students in the 4th–10th grades are involved in ecological studies and water quality monitoring throughout the Budd/Deschutes Watershed in South Puget Sound (Meyer 1997).

Getting Started: Sample Activities

The following are several activities to illustrate how to foster the natural intelligence in the classroom. There is an example for each grade level: elementary, middle, and high school. These samples illustrate how easy it is to target the naturalist intelligence in different areas of study. Instructors can use these examples to spark ideas for their own units, or they can refer to the original source for complete instructions.

Cooperative Learning for the Naturalist Intelligence: Elementary School

The following is a lesson from a unit on Understanding Ecosystems from the fourth grade science curriculum in the Southfield Public Schools, Southfield, Michigan. Students work in cooperative groups, researching the answer to the focus question: What is the relationship between spiders and insects? The students also make a prediction of what this relationship might be before the investigation begins.

To begin, students discuss the differences between insects and spiders. Then students capture several spiders and insects around their home in one container and several spiders and insects around their school in another container.

In cooperative groups, students observe the external structure of each insect and spider. The group picks an artist to make a detailed drawing of each insect and spider and to label the body parts. Using reference books from the library, students can check the accuracy of their drawings and labels and make corrections and additions if necessary.

After recording the behavior of the insects and the spiders for at least a week, the class discusses their findings. Each student can then write a summary of his/her investigation, answering these questions: Was his or her prediction supported or not supported? What did he or she learn?

Thematic Learning for the Naturalist Intelligence: Middle School

This example is for the middle school level but, by using different levels of ecological literature, it can be adapted to both the elementary and the high school levels. This idea comes from the article "Good Science, by George!" in the November/December 1994 issue of *Science Scope,* written by Jean Pottle, an instructor at Mid-State College in Auburn, Maine.

The theme is ecological mysteries, and the activities use three pieces of literature by Jean Craighead George. The first, *Who Really Killed Cock Robin?,* was originally published in 1971 and reissued in 1991. The second, *The Missing 'Gator of Gumbo Limbo,* was published in 1992, and the third of the ecological mysteries, *The Fire Bug Connection,* was published in 1993. All three of these books lend themselves to an interdisciplinary study of the ecosystem.

> **All three of these books lend themselves to an interdisciplinary study of the ecosystem.**

The story *Who Really Killed Cock Robin?* is about a town called Saddleboro that prides itself on environmental awareness. To the chagrin of town officials, the community encounters many environmental problems, including an ant infestation, the deaths of two birds, and an absence of frogs and fish in the nearby river. Middle schooler Tony Isadora becomes an environmental Sherlock Holmes to discover the causes of the problems, modeling his approach to problem solving after that of his scientist brother.

The student reads the novel and uses his/her textbook as a reference. The science teacher uses the topics of histochemistry, dioxin poisoning, insecticides, nitrogen, lead, sulfur dioxide, and parasites, to name a few, as an interesting way to introduce the students to ecosystems and pollution. An English teacher can concentrate on character development and the relationships between the characters in the novel or examine the importance of journal- or record-keeping in problem solving. A social studies teacher can focus on the relationships between the town's citizens and administrators, raising issues such as the importance of being actively involved with local issues, the need for careful evaluation of the news, the importance of long-range damage—those who caused the pollution, those who stood by and let it happen, or both. (See Figure 6.)

The second novel, *The Missing 'Gator of Gumbo Limbo,* set in the Everglades, can be a great starting point for a study of the plants and animals of the tropic zone. The mystery in the novel centers on the disap-

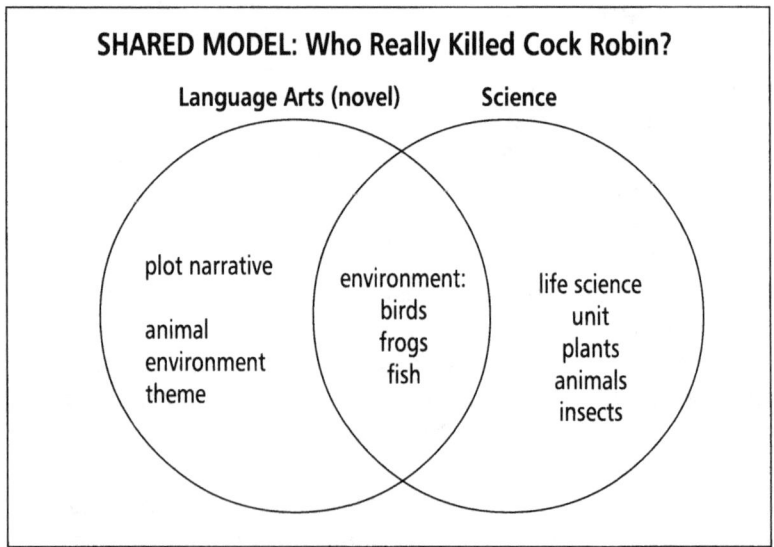

SHARED MODEL: Who Really Killed Cock Robin?

Language Arts (novel)   Science

plot narrative

animal environment theme

environment: birds frogs fish

life science unit plants animals insects

(Adapted from *The Mindful School: How to Integrate the Curricula,* Robin Fogarty, 1991)

FIGURE 6

pearance of Dajon, an alligator who helps keep the waters of Gumbo Limbo clean. Throughout the novel, the author emphasizes the interdependence of one small ecosystem and then expands her view to include the problems that humans' entry into the Everglades has caused. The character of Priscilla, the poet, can be developed in the English curriculum and social studies students can study a group of homeless people who seek shelter in Gumbo Limbo. (See Figure 7.)

The third ecological mystery, *The Fire Bug Connection,* is the story of Maggie Mercer, a middle school student who is fascinated by all animals, especially insects. Maggie investigates the world of spiders, bombadier beetles, wasps, bats, and a collection of fire bugs. The trouble is, the fire bugs never reach maturity, leaving Maggie and her friends with the mystery of what kills the fire bugs before they reach maturity.

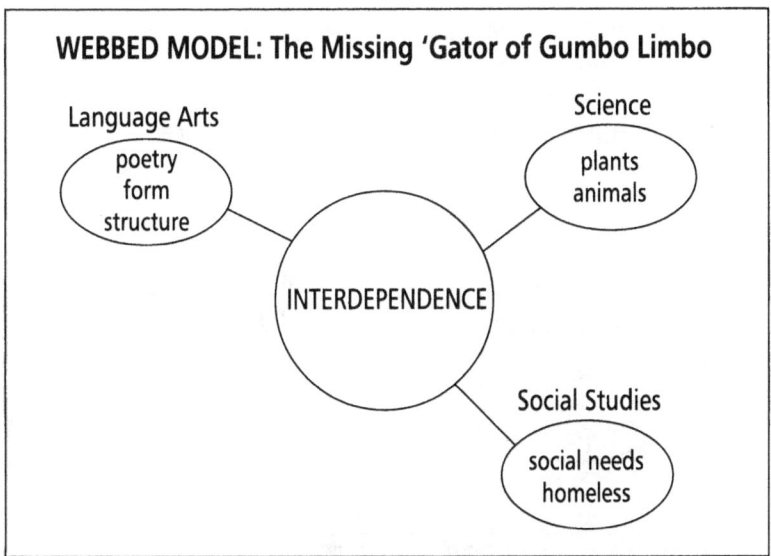

WEBBED MODEL: The Missing 'Gator of Gumbo Limbo

Language Arts
poetry
form
structure

Science
plants
animals

INTERDEPENDENCE

Social Studies
social needs
homeless

(Adapted from *The Mindful School: How to Integrate the Curricula,* Robin Fogarty, 1991)

FIGURE 7

The book provides an easy entry to a study of the animal world. Many little-known scientific facts are presented. The English teacher can explore the changing relationships of the characters as they try to solve the mystery, as well as how the author tells an interesting story while broadening the reader's scientific knowledge. The social studies teacher can look at relationships between parents and children and how common interests make family life more interesting and exciting. (See Figure 8.)

The use of an ecological mystery in literature lends itself to the format of the thematic learning unit. Students can choose one of the three books, based on their particular interest. The students can work in cooperative groups to brainstorm a list of questions that forces them to address the theme's critical issues and come up with a hook question/statement that

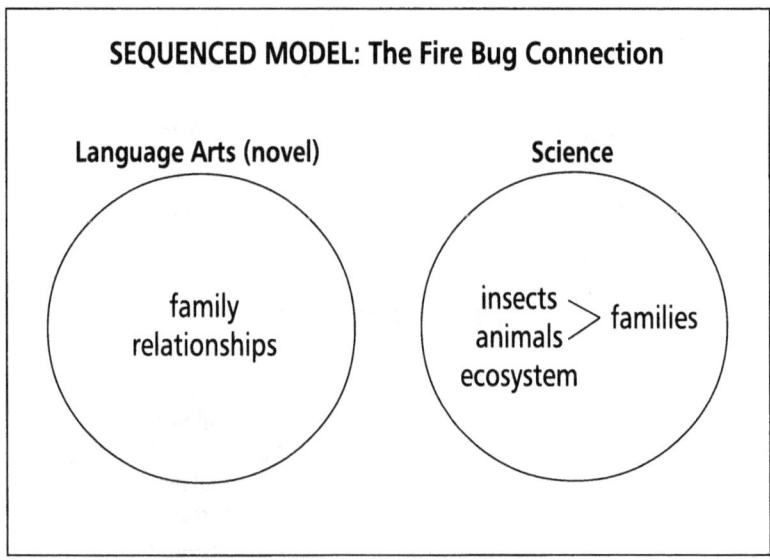

(Adapted from *The Mindful School: How to Integrate the Curricula*, Robin Fogarty, 1991)

FIGURE 8

drives their problem-solving effort (e.g., Ecological Mysteries: Becoming a Scientific Detective).

The theme is turned into a problem-solving investigation. The theme can be webbed, shared, or sequenced (see *The Mindful School: How to Integrate the Curricula* for a description and explanation of how to use these models) to the different disciplines, as suggested above with the English and social studies teachers. In addition, students can choose from a variety of activities from the multiple intelligences grid (see Figure 2). Students then engage in the problem-solving process of gathering facts, analyzing the problem, generating alternatives, and advocating a solution or position.

> **The theme can be webbed, shared, or sequenced to the different disciplines . . .**

Problem-Based Learning for the Naturalist Intelligence: High School

The following is a description of an air quality analysis project that Nancy Kawecki Nega, eighth grade general science teacher at Churchville Junior High School in Elmhurst, Illinois, did with her students. She won the 1995 Presidential Award in secondary science. The project is described in the article, "Analyzing Air Quality," in the February 1997 issue of *Science Scope.* Here the project has been adapted for the high school level.

KleenAirCo requests the help of students to come up with a device to measure air pollution. The objective of the activity is for students to research information on air pollution, form groups to create a device to measure air pollution, and create a proposal for their air monitoring device that they will submit to KleenAirCo.

To begin, students consult textbooks, library reference books, magazine articles, electronic encyclopedias, and the Internet, as well as any other resources they can find for information on pollution. After researching, students report what they know about air pollution in general and indoor air pollution specifically. The report should include what air pollution is, what causes it, the different types, ways to measure it, and known or suspected health concerns. At the end of the report, students should state what they would like to learn by doing this project.

> **... students should state what they would like to learn by doing this project.**

Students then organize into groups, and each group creates a concept map using information from all the reports. This helps the groups brainstorm ideas for how to design the experiment and decide which ideas are workable. The groups need to consider how and where they will measure air quality and for how long. They also need to consider how they will collect and display their data.

Students' final proposals should include all the steps they are going to take in conducting their experiments, a materials list, a labeled drawing of the air-monitoring device, a complete list of references, and a short biography of each person on the research team.

Once the proposals are accepted, the groups can build their monitors and carry out the experiment. Students organize and graph all their data and then write a complete report analyzing and explaining the results of the experiment. Students should also include a final labeled illustration of their monitor.

At the conclusion of this project, students can present their work and results at an air pollution conference. Each group can display their work, results, and recommendations. Students should be prepared to answer questions from the other groups.

Other Ideas to Foster the Naturalist Intelligence

As mentioned with the above activities, these are ideas to get teachers started with thinking about the naturalist intelligence. Educators can adapt these ideas to their own grade levels and units of study or they can refer to the original source for step-by-step instructions.

It's a Seed of an Idea

This activity comes from *Problem-Based Learning and Other Curriculum Models for the Multiple Intelligences Classroom.* It was originally intended for the elementary school level, but it can be easily adapted to the middle and high school levels.

The activity begins with the teacher selecting a topic to brainstorm, such as plants. Students come up with a whole list of ideas including living and growing things, family trees, seeds, etc. The teacher then poses several questions focusing in on the topic of family trees. The following are some sample questions: What is a family? What is a tree? What is a family tree? Can you grow a family tree? etc. From the questioning, a theme title emerges, Growing and the Family Tree: Where Are Your Roots? The topic can be adapted to several areas of study (see Figure 9). All of the intelligences can be tapped with this one theme, including the naturalist (see Figure 10).

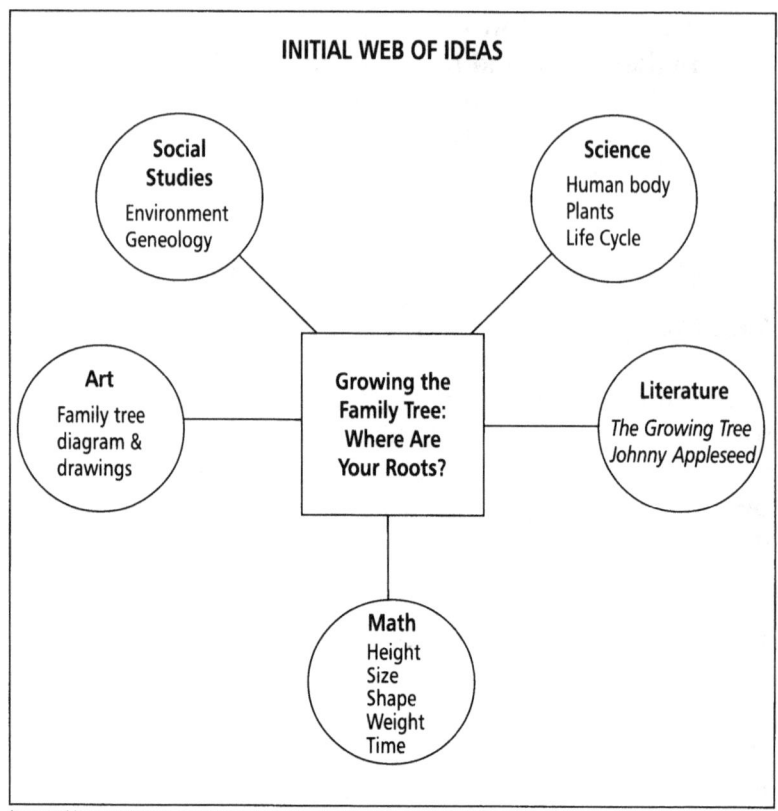

INITIAL WEB OF IDEAS

Social Studies
Environment
Geneology

Science
Human body
Plants
Life Cycle

Art
Family tree
diagram &
drawings

Growing the Family Tree: Where Are Your Roots?

Literature
The Growing Tree
Johnny Appleseed

Math
Height
Size
Shape
Weight
Time

(From *Problem-Based Learning and Other Curriculum Models,* Robin Fogarty, 1997)

FIGURE 9

Jagged Profile Activities: Naturalist Intelligence

This activity is one activity in a group of activities called Jagged Profiles in *Integrating Curricula With Multiple Intelligences: Teams, Themes and Threads.*

Students are shown a set of tracks divided into three frames. Older students can actually go outside and find a set of tracks to draw in the three-frame format. This also incorporates other intelligences such as the bodily

Multiple Intelligences Grid of Activities
Growing & the Family Tree: Where Are the Roots?

Visual	Verbal	Logical	Musical	Bodily	Interpersonal	Intrapersonal	Naturalist
Slides or microscope	Reading diaries, journals from family	Graphing growth of self; plants; family	Music of various generations	Planting seedling	Interviewing parents	Geneology: family tree w/pictures	Growing beans
Pictures of growing things	Writing about "family roots"	Diagraming family tree	Growing plants to music	Nature walk	Interviewing grandparents	Journal of investigation	Growing grass
Family videos	Keeping a plant growth log	Surveys, statistics, data & information about plants, or families, etc.	Nature music (waves, wind, birds)	"Hug"-a-tree unit	Small group research projects	Diary of growth	Planting a garden
Photograph albums	Telling about family heritage		Music of various cultural heritages	Exploring attic, closets, cellars, for family heirlooms, etc.	Group murals of pond, rain forest, field, etc.	Log of learning about family	Tracing natural life cycle in pond
Sketching family members		DNA—% of inherited traits, family pedigree	Performing music of an era	Role-playing family heroes	Partner work on projects	Scrapbook	Hatching butterflies
Illustrations of plant parts, etc.	Old newspapers, yearbooks, scrapbooks	Demographic information	Appreciating music of a region		Relating to others in family history	Portfolio	Raising tadpoles to frogs
Mapping a flower garden	Listening to family stories; oral histories					Reflective quotes for sayings from family	"Adopting" a tree
Films of other generations							Studying rain forests for life cycles

(From *Problem-Based Learning & Other Curriculum Models for the Multiple Intelligences Classroom,* Robin Fogarty, 1997)

FIGURE 10

and the visual. The teacher can then choose all or several of the illustrations to use in class.

The teacher shows the whole class the illustration one step at a time. Then students can make observations and inferences for each frame. For example, using the illustration in Figure 11, a student may make the following observations and inferences:

Frame 1
Observations: (1) there are two sets of tracks, (2) one set is larger than the other, (3) they appear to be converging
Inferences: (1) one is a bear, one is a duck, (2) the tracks were left at the same time, (3) they are tracks in the snow

Frame 2
Observations: (1) the tracks converge, (2) the tracks are in a random pattern, (3) the tracks are mixed up
Inferences: (1) the animals were fighting, (2) they were mating, (3) they were marking the same spot at different times

Frame 3
Observations: (1) there is one set of tracks, (2) the larger tracks remain, (3) the smaller tracks have disappeared
Inferences: (1) one animal ate the other (survival of the fittest), (2) one carried the other (friendship theory), (3) one flew away (escapist theory)

Younger students can then turn their observations and inferences into a short story with illustrations. Older students can research different animals and tracks to verify the validity of some of their inferences. Again, these activities draw upon the naturalist as well as other intelligences.

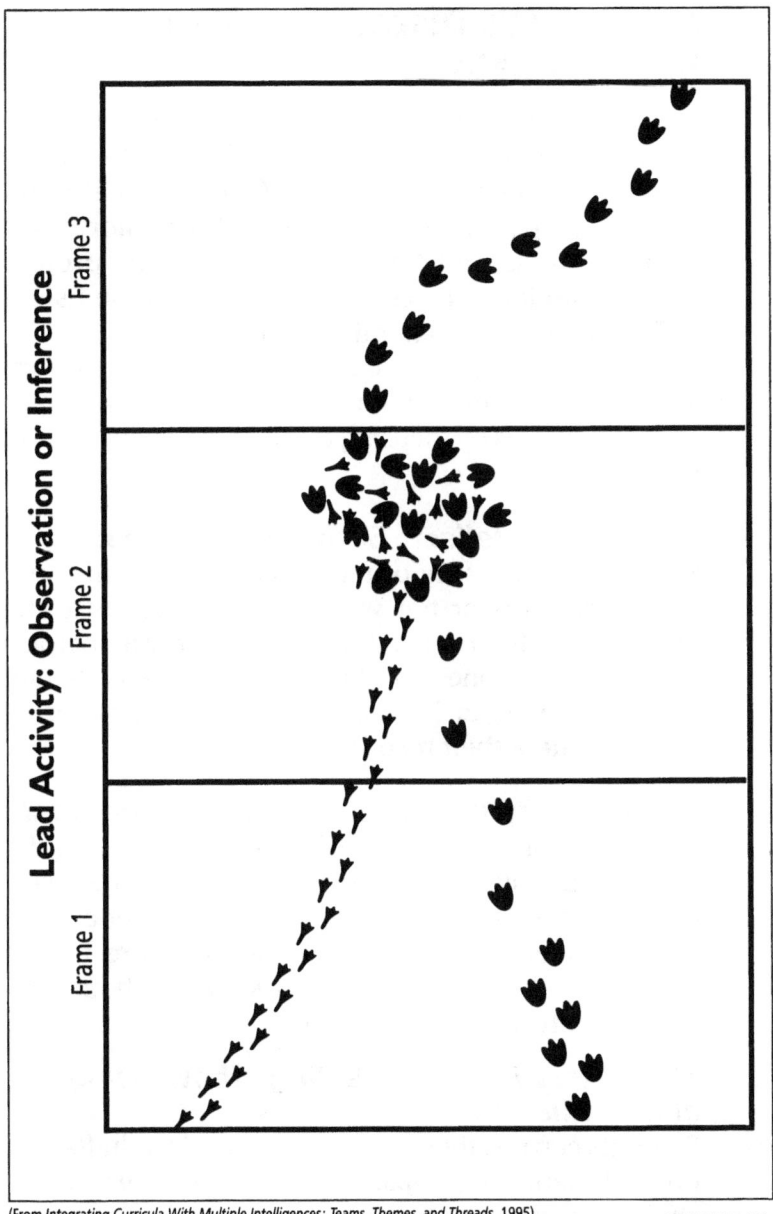

Lead Activity: Observation or Inference

Frame 1   Frame 2   Frame 3

(From *Integrating Curricula With Multiple Intelligences: Teams, Themes, and Threads,* 1995)

FIGURE 11

A Scientist's Discoveries About Human Anatomy

This activity is from *Project Learning for the Multiple Intelligences Classroom.* It uses the Three-Story Intellect With Multiple Intelligences (see Figure 12) and includes projects that range from basic first-story tasks to more advanced third-story tasks. This project involves students in scientific inquiry and the use of skills related to the naturalist intelligence.

The purpose of this activity is for students to learn the basic structure and functions of the human body. Students do this by focusing on Nobel Prize winners in medicine.

First-Story Intellect: Gathering Information

Students begin by choosing a Nobel Prize winner and researching his or her work. Students can use the library or the Internet or they can interview a doctor, a nurse, or someone who knows about the particular Nobel Prize winner. It's important for students to properly document their resources.

Second-Story Intellect: Focusing on the Goal

Depending on the grade level, teachers can make the goal of the project to create a medical pamphlet illustrating and explaining the Nobel Prize winner and his or her research or to create a birthday card for the scientist. Individually or in groups, students should create a prototype of their project.

Third-Story Intellect: Testing, Showcasing, and Evaluating

Students can test their prototypes by trading drafts with other students or groups. After this reviewing process, students can create the final version of their projects.

The Three-Story Intellect
With Multiple Intelligences

3
APPLYING

Verbal: using metaphors, similes, analogies, puns, plays on words
Visual: visualizing, imagining, dreaming, envisioning, symbolizing
Logical: evaluating, judging, refining, creating analogies, reasoning, critiquing
Musical: composing, improvising, critiquing, performing, conducting
Bodily: constructing, dramatizing, performing, experimenting, sculpting
Interpersonal: debating, compromising, mediating, arbitrating
Intrapersonal: mediating, intuiting, innovating, inventing, creating
Naturalist: forecasting, predicting, interrelating, synthesizing, categorizing

PROCESSING Crystallize Ideas

Verbal: paraphrasing, essay writing, labeling, reporting, organizing
Visual: sketching, mapping, diagramming, illustrating, cartooning
Logical: graphing, comparing, classifying, ranking, analyzing, coding
Musical: playing, selecting, singing, responding to music
Bodily: rehearsing, studying, experimenting, investigating
Interpersonal: expressing, telling/retelling, arguing, discussing
Intrapersonal: studying, self-assessing, interpreting, processing
Naturalist: categorizing, sorting, relating, classifying

GATHERING Research Project

Verbal: questioning, reading, listing, telling, writing, finding, listening, documenting
Visual: viewing, observing, seeing, describing, showing
Logical: recording, collecting, logging, documenting
Musical: listening, gathering, audiotaping, attending concerts
Bodily: preparing, exploring, investigating, interviewing
Interpersonal: interacting, teaming, interviewing, affirming
Intrapersonal: reflecting, expressing, reacting, journaling
Naturalist: observing, catching, identifying, photographing

(Adapted from *Problem-Based Learning & Other Curriculum Models for the Multiple Intelligences Classroom*, Robin Fogarty, 1997)

FIGURE 12

The projects can then be showcased for the class and even the rest of the school. The teacher can then use a rubric to make sure the students have met all the criteria set at the beginning of the project.

The Naturalist Intelligence Put to Use

As we learn more about the naturalist intelligence, it is clear that many teachers have been using and teaching the tools of this intelligence all along. With its addition to the list of multiple intelligence, it causes teachers to be more purposeful in designing learning experiences that address the skills of this intelligence. It also helps teachers find ways to engage the naturalist child with that special topic or project from the natural world that excites and challenges. In closing, this information adds to the knowledge base about how children learn and provides additional learning tools, strategies, and opportunities to understand and reach more children.

References

Bellanca, James. 1997. *Active Learning Handbook for the Multiple Intelligences Classroom.* Arlington Heights, IL: SkyLight Training and Publishing, Inc.

Berman, Sally. 1997. *Project Learning for the Multiple Intelligences Classroom.* Arlington Heights, IL: SkyLight Training and Publishing, Inc.

Chapman, Carolyn. 1993. *If the Shoe Fits . . .: How to Develop Multiple Intelligences in the Classroom.* Arlington Heights, IL: IRI/SkyLight Training and Publishing, Inc.

Checkley, K. 1997. The First Seven . . . and the Eighth: A Conversation with Howard Gardner. *Educational Leadership,* September: 8–13.

Fogarty, Robin. 1991. *The Mindful School: How to Integrate the Curricula.* Arlington Heights, IL: IRI/SkyLight Training and Publishing, Inc.

Fogarty, Robin. 1997. *Brain Compatible Classrooms.* Arlington Heights, IL: SkyLight Training and Publishing, Inc.

Fogarty, Robin. 1997. *Problem-Based Learning & Other Curriculum Models: For the Multiple Intelligences Classroom.* Arlington Heights, IL: IRI/SkyLight Training and Publishing, Inc.

Fogarty, Robin and Judy Stoehr. 1995. *Integrating Curricula With Multiple Intelligences: Teams, Themes & Threads.* Arlington Heights, IL: IRI/SkyLight Training and Publishing, Inc.

Gardner, Howard. 1983. *Frames of Mind: The Theory of Multiple Intelligences.* New York: Basic Books.

Gardner, Howard. 1993. *Multiple Intelligences: The Theory in Practice.* New York: Basic Books.

George, Jean Craighead. 1971. *Who Really Killed Cock Robin?* New York: HarperCollins.

George, Jean Craighead. 1992. *The Missing 'Gator of Gumbo Limbo.* New York: HarperCollins.

George, Jean Craighead. 1993. *The Fire Bug Connection.* New York: HarperCollins.

Lazear, David. 1991. *Seven Ways of Knowing: Teaching for Multiple Intelligences, 2nd ed.* Arlington Heights, IL: IRI/ SkyLight Training and Publishing, Inc.

Lazear, David. 1991. *Seven Ways of Teaching: The Artistry of Teaching With Multiple Intelligences, 2nd ed.* Arlington Heights, IL: IRI/SkyLight Training and Publishing, Inc.

Meyer, Maggie. 1997. The GREENing of Learning: Using the Eighth Intelligence. *Educational Leadership,* September: 32–34.

O'Connor, Anna and Sheila Callahan-Young. 1994. *Seven Windows to a Child's World.* Arlington Heights, IL: IRI/ SkyLight Training and Publishing, Inc.

Pottle, Jean. 1994. "Good Science, by George!" *Science Scope,* November/December.

Notes

Notes

There are
one-story intellects,
two-story intellects, and three-story
intellects with skylights. All fact collectors, who
have no aim beyond their facts, are one-story men. Two-story men
compare, reason, generalize, using the labors of the fact collectors as
well as their own. Three-story men idealize, imagine,
predict—their best illumination comes from
above, through the skylight.

—*Oliver Wendell*
Holmes

Training and Publishing Inc.

In compliance with GPSR, should you have any concerns about the safety of this product, please advise: International Associates Auditing & Certification Limited The Black Church, St Mary's Place, Dublin 7, D07 P4AX Ireland EUAR@ie.ia-net.com

www.ingramcontent.com/pod-product-compliance
Lightning Source LLC
Jackson TN
JSHW080038010226
97517JS00015B/163